Solar Flares

Kaitlyn G. Hall

BookLeaf Publishing

India | USA | UK

Presentation by *BookLeaf Publishing*

Web: www.bookleafpub.com

E-mail: info@bookleafpub.com

ISBN: 9789360941277

First edition 2024

For Emily Grace Hart, my best friend for eternity, and for those who have experienced a lost or interrupted connection in their life.

ACKNOWLEDGEMENT

I would like to thank my writing mentor, Marta Lane, who has inspired me to continue writing and dive deeper into my passion for poetry. I would also like to thank my best friend, Emily, who has been there for me since childhood. You have brought joy and light into my life and have supported every one of my endeavors. I cannot wait to grow and connect with others through my writing and improve over the course of my life.

PREFACE

Many feel as though they should gain control of their lives and who they meet, but the world does not work like that. We should live in the comfort of life taking its own course and giving the universe the reins. Similar to how solar flares affect Earth and the internet, Solar Flares aims to find new perspectives and tells stories based around missed or interrupted connections. The lost connections could be physical, mental, social, or the link between life and death. A missed connection could be caused by an action, a thought, a decision, the way of the world, or some other unworldly cause. It could be a missed chance or missed opportunity. Overall, I enjoyed the writing process and I hope that my poetry will inspire others to understand the way of the world through poetry.

Never Have I Been Given Flowers

I have never been given flowers
Not the pretty bouquets wrapped in bows,
the single potted orchid or even the cliché rose.
My hopes are in for the surprise and the handoff
to my shaking heart

At first glance, a pink flower is all you see,
but underneath I am a cactus, whose love is
prickly
You keep watering me with affection and
attention,
but I don't grow like that.
I cannot dismantle my skin down to my genetics

Not that I deserve what is grown in the garden
but I will settle for anything
The apples from the tree you've taken years to
grow may be more bountiful,
but to give me such priceless produce is unwise.
I will bite into it with no regard for its taste, my
only intention is to see how bitter it must be.

Maybe I do not deserve the flowers, or the
constant watering, or the apples of your harvest:

I worry that you will not come back to me the
day I am finally ready for your love.
So I continue to eat and spit out the ripe fruits of
others
to ensure that I will never have to feel what I
thought I felt with you again.

I, The Sun and You, The Moon

Together, we work to keep our little Earth alive,
friends for more than four billion years defined.
The large star that brightens your day every
night,
even though we sit adjacent on the Earth's
skyline.

Behind the scenes, you avail my light to be seen
and you shine to all of the wandering eyes
You lead the lost and the blind,
but one day my fire will no longer ignite.

You favor Venus and Mars,
those who orbit closest to home.
You prefer the company of the afar stars,
obscure lights with short but alluring lives.

And time and time again, you come back for the
ellipse
You are reminded of my importance to keep our
friendship existent
No matter the one hundred and fifty million
kilometer distance,
you will see me once again to apologize.

The Fuchsia Fox and the Calico Cat

Carmine pigment and splotches of ink splatters
the fur
and his mate wears white caked with black and
orange.
Hopping over one another in a motion blur in the
field,

knocking over the feline, the fox runs off.
Frustrated and hissy, the cat gets lost and looks
through the evergreen, joining in this game of
hide and seek.

In a flash, a crackle and a bang hit the night sky
and whiskers tracing the dirt become drenched
in blood.
At the end of the trail, the fox had been shot:
Another friend is lost before the morning sun.

Denim-Blue Waters

5

The broken disco ball rests in sand like a
deflated beach ball, cheaply purchased online
A cocktail lover sips on beer whilst sitting by the
shoreline,
her old cowboy hat tilted downward towards the
denim-blue waters.
I fetch a blanket from the vessel for her
shoulders like she was a helpless pauper,
only to come back to no one perched on the
beach's borderline.

The Golden Rays of My Childhood

The sun use to light up the trees and the
pavement with its golden rays
The world was so warm in the past,
I taught myself how to hopscotch over the lines
of the sidewalks
Cheap markers smudged the bottom of my
hands,
then they cupped over the rollie pollies hiding in
the grass.
Shown in the shower of the sprinklers were
rainbows.

Now life is a black and white film,
we drink in red, plastic cups
and the liquor stains our livers.
I learn how to live my life away from home,
the world is disconnecting from my youth
and the moon glows dimly on this night.

Yellow Peonies Live Longer Than You Did

By tradition, I visit you annually,
your favorite yellow peonies placed by your
headstone
Flowers live longer in graveyards than in the
warm hands of a lover,
I want to dig under the dirt and let my fingertips
find yours

Old acquaintances of yours came to the party,
I learned a new song for you, it is called Not All
Who Wander Are Lost
The dirt underneath my fingernails make playing
the strings like picking up coins on a slick
surface
and your acquaintances do not mind my singing,
as they do not truly know me.

Some of your co-workers clocked in to your
deathday,
their eyes pry behind me, looking into my feeble
entries.
My dark thoughts are hidden with scribbles and
bad penmanship
When they left, I gave you my notes and letters.

Your best friend went to visit today,
a dog loyal to its owner.
He could smell through my search-and-rescue
mission,
yet he only stared at me and sighed at the sight
of our old photographs

Your family came to see you earlier,
they were not too happy to be a witness to my
resolution.
My fingers tremble on the board, your whispers
blow the candles out,
they barely give you enough strength to speak to
me.

Every year, I will bring the yellow peonies, bury
the guitar pick, write you the letters, burn your
old photographs, and talk to you through the
oujia board.
As the years go by, one by one they stop coming
by,
and I will still come and say my miss you's,
goodbye.

Plastered Missing Posters on the Corner Store Window

Autumn's golden leaves fall,
a casual stroll down to the corner store
I plaster a missing poster on the tinted glass,
smoothing out the creases on the flyer that's not
even allowed.

Playing on the swings were the last time I saw
you: the extrovert with a passion to explore.
We use to walk down after school to the by-pass,
your gentle fingers intertwined in mine, your
hair floating above the clouds.

I knew it would not last for long and I foresaw
you leaving through the school door.
I thought that I could find you on my own,
perhaps
we could meet once more and rekindle the
friendship, endowed.

So I asked around town to see where you had
gone:
A friend said she saw you walking against the
downpour,

and an elderly lady on the street does not know,
she snaps.
We promise we will find her, the cops vowed.

You went somewhere else beyond,
but I sent you a message that in hopes you do
not ignore.
You have one new message! My computer dings
and my legs collapse
From the corner store: A wide sale is happening
now, get here before the crowd!

I cut the line of the utility pole

Copper against the glove-compartment hatchet,
the pole invades the thicket from the deep cut
Softwood splinters into ample fragments,
and it plummets onto our truck still stuck in the
rut

A fire could arise, that was stupid and
dangerous, warns the law.
"Sorry officer, we just don't know what got into
him"
We snicker to ourselves, the five of us tipsy and
on withdrawals,
steel cuffs our wrists, and all account of a
drunken whim

You Should Have Kissed Me One Last Time

Dear love of my life, or ex-lover rather,
Read me like a newspaper, the latest events
carried in my posture.
I hate the way you focus on the reflections
instead of what is in the lake
You must need spectacles to notice how I yearn
for you
Blind to the swan ballet, you dismiss my fervor
in that single moment.

A stray dog, you fled without considering my
love or care
Didn't you feel it too? The heat, the pressure,
my dejection.
My frustration revealed in my veins from your
sorrow expressions
You should have kissed me one last time,
instead, you left me an apology letter of false
hope.

I understand the reason why you skipped the
stone in the water and looked for better ones,
if that is what you wish then I can allow our past
to drown in vain.

If the Satellites Fall

If all else fails, do not let the satellites fall,
as they guide us to our eventual destination.
No interference can intrude on the map of
interrelations,
we are born to be escorted by fate.

I only hope that the man-made stars will
continuously steer you to me
but there are rules within the universe that piece
us all together:
Never try to force a connection, you will end up
breaking it that way.
The gravitational pull of the soul ties would die,
if the satellites fall.

Missed Calls From the Apartment Complex

Neon lights fight the rain on the coastal city-side
Our living quarters garnished, yet it presumes as
abandoned.
Trees branches knock on the glass, calling for
me as a ghost would.

Torn textile and grooves sit on the cushions
The couch arranged infront of the wall's sun
stain,
where the bargain TV use to reside

In the midst of our relationship, you got rid of
our TV
The grapevine said you sold it to a pawn shop
for me,
thanks to my addiction to the motion screen
alike yours to the cigarettes .

Glancing at my phone, still no messages from
you
You missed twenty one calls from me,
they break in my vigor and vehemence, they
both coincide.

My leather jacket has been missing for
sometime,
you took it as a reminder of me to carry
wherever you go,
I believe that you must of left for the East Coast.

Similar to the boxed TV from an auction,
I will discover you again engulfed in shells and
seaweed.
One day you will wash back to me from the tide:
I do not deserve to raze your rising fire so I will
stay stationed at my post for now.

The Day My Freedom Was Taken From Me

My freedom was taken from me the day I grew
frisky
Screeching, stopping, stomping, hissing,
scraping
From explorer to prisoner, the gravel vs the cold
metal container
Claws hooked on cages confused, new faces
surround me

The ones in green are the scariest, they slam the
doors
Please leave me alone, I was just fine on my
own.
They pace around endlessly, shuffling their
papers
I do not wish to breathe in this world of urine
and eye-watering bleach

Little fingers of warmth, prying at my whiskers
and my paws
Pushing myself into my corner of solidarity to
escape, you laugh
Nimble, you tease me, and I pounce. And
a violent sound comes out of your mouth

You are dragged away of my grasp, goodbye
baby powder
Observe as the cage next to me is ajar:
The unknown fur balls rustle inbetween one
another,
a kitten is picked up and taken past the big door

My neighbor, the mama, cries but is too
overwhelmed to fight back,
as the days pass by, more of her little fur balls
disappear.
Her eyes say she can no longer do anything,
she's exhausted.
The nights grow colder for her, our thinning fur
is what is left of us

I keep her snug through the spaces in our cages:
She misses her absent babies, we share a mutual
grievance.
The last few days have been empty, less come
through the slamming door
Until a worker drapped in black drags her away,
departing behind the counter.

Her screams are like waves, they crash and then
they calm until there is smooth glass
As more days pass, I feel as though I will never
truly live again,

I pin for the world, the trees, the dirt, and
surprisingly enough, affection.
The smell of bleach and baby powder fills my
lungs.

I cannot move anymore. There is no point.
The one in black keeps passing by my corridor
I want to go home, let me go home. I told him.
Then rattles open my prison cell, I panic

No energy to push back, he scoops me up and
takes me away from my cell
The ice cold table, the hands, the needle, the
ejection, the peace.
I beg the man, "Why do you feel the need to
'rescue me?'"
The day my freedom was taken from me, was
the day that I had signed over my life.

Addicted to the High

I eat the dirt every time.
We love the pain, we love the high
Wrestle your own friends to the ground.
Just go back in a year,
it's not running, it's escaping
Your mother does not have to know.

Her daughter is missing,
awaiting a phone call is her mother.
There is no note, just an empty teenager's bed,
a bedroom filled with dust-coated things from an
ex eight year old.
The mother sobbed every night that she was
gone
and her heart stopped before her sun came back.

An Ode to the Demise of Us (and the rest of the world)

Oh, the demise of us, and the rest of the world.
The collective finally has a common reason to
fight for the last flight as bacteria does for
survival,
but my love holds my arm patiently like ivy,
bittersweet melancholia
The unfortunate give into the onslaught while
others shed terror, gathering in flocks.

Oh, the demise of us, and the rest of the world.
My love's sultry tears burn unlike the dying sun;
Yet our love is supernatural, no matter the
circumstances, I told her,
I promise to come back as a star and search for
you in the rubble.

Oh, the demise of us, and the rest of the world.
We watch the sun's last set like it was the movie
we watched on our first date
and at last, our eyes connect. A signal that we
are ready, so we pull off our oxygen masks
and we kiss one final time as the tainted air kills
us on The Final Day of Earth.

Strangers and Dance Floors

The rain crashes onto the apartment window,
beige walls and the convenience store artwork
feel vacant and desolate.
They say where you go represents what your
heart desires

Twenty one missed calls and I still can't pull
myself together to answer you
I love you to the furthest reaches of our
expanding universe
You were my soulmate, but I crave strangers and
dance floors.

I have lost my passion once again as the moon
loses its entirety on occasions,
I've spilled your love for me, an over-the-brim
cup of coffee.
I do not deserve you, yet I miss your strange
addictions.

One Head, Two Bodies

We had lost a head,
two into one, sewn at once.
One head on two bears

It's Complicated Yellow

At the party we were invited to,
the foyer had set out multi-colored cups, each
representing your status
Like a stoplight, you must respect the rules of
the road:
Never intrude on red, be careful before yellow,
and go for it with green

Already Taken Red:
There is a couple drinking out of the crimson
cups and making out in the kitchen.
Her merlot painted lips smudge the glasses,
drinking sangria
His fingers hooked around her garnet necklace
as he makes her face burgundy

It's Complicated Yellow:
I imagine us as saffron, almost red but
commonly seen as yellow.
At the entryway, I pick the honey cup: In hopes
that our relationship blooms like dandelions and
does not turn salty like mustard.
Butterscotch hue reminds me of how sweet you
are to me.

Ready to Go Green:
But as I watch as you pick venom green and my
vision of you melts into sour lime:
My lucky shamrock turned out to be just grass.
So, I left the party with a shiny new emerald
color.

I hate the internet.

25

Social consumption is social media,
I hate the internet.
Click left, swipe right

Give me the past, the hope, and it's love letters:
I want to sing time traveler blues out-of-tune.
Solar flares take them out!

If not, I will do it myself and break open the
router,
then go out with a baseball bat and smash the
internet tower.
You have lost connection!

Enamor

I am in love with you and I do not know why,
be careful with my love as it does not come and
go for everyone.
You will break my heart, don't

If I rush into these feelings, my car goes
spinning into the brick wall
Even though patience hurts, I will keep a steady
and slow hand on the portrait
You are the infection in my brain that pauses my
ticking clock.

I am in love with you and I do not know why,
do not tease me with hopefulness and
forgiveness. I promise that I will fall off this cliff
with you,
but you must take the first step and I will
provide the parachute.

Please catch me before my flight at the airport:
I know what I feel, it is
this mysterious feeling called enamor.

Running Out of Oxygen

The clues cannot simply be stitched together,
they must be bait on a reel first
Unfortunately, the red string that ties the case
through and through is limited,
They are running out of strings to fish with.
The puzzle was similar to a chess game: but the
knight is unknown and the queen has been
murdered
His wife beside him, she moves the photos and
the red string across the cork board:
The weapon, the suspects, the scene, the maps
marked with locations
The wife's words keep on making him sail off
course however,
little did the detective know that he should have
been searching his wife's ring finger instead.

There is an answer, a treasure, hidden
underneath the rocks and seashells
Somewhere in the sand, a key is buried
The detective is drowning in false statements
and struggling to find the shark in the schools of
fishes.
The sailors on the surface desire to know what is
in the chest

and the scuba diver is under pressure
The time running out and the amount of
oxygen in the tank is getting lower by the
minute.

Yet the scuba diver never witnessed the shark's
friend, the manta ray, swimming besides him,
he never figured out that it was the manta ray
who tossed the key away in the first place.

Solar Flares Severed the Landline

Solar flares severed the landline,
the call interrupted by the sun's flames.
Death bends its metal keys,
no longer able to enter the secret garden.

The hermit tossed the coin into the well,
gambling his worth for an eager wish.
Love breaks its lost string every time,
casting its magnetic connection to the side.

www.ingramcontent.com/pod-product-compliance
Lightning Source LLC
LaVergne TN
LVHW010952200726

843509LV00013B/2391